SNAPPING TURTLES

BY SHANNON JADE

Apex is distributed by North Star Editions:
sales@northstareditions.com | 888-417-0195

Produced for Apex by Red Line Editorial.

Photographs ©: Shutterstock Images, cover, 1, 6–7, 10–11, 12–13, 14–15, 16–17, 18, 19, 20, 22–23, 24, 25, 26–27, 29; iStockphoto, 4–5, 8–9

Library of Congress Control Number: 2022920182

ISBN
978-1-63738-549-4 (hardcover)
978-1-63738-603-3 (paperback)
978-1-63738-708-5 (ebook pdf)
978-1-63738-657-6 (hosted ebook)

Printed in the United States of America
Mankato, MN
082023

NOTE TO PARENTS AND EDUCATORS

Apex books are designed to build literacy skills in striving readers. Exciting, high-interest content attracts and holds readers' attention. The text is carefully leveled to allow students to achieve success quickly. Additional features, such as bolded glossary words for difficult terms, help build comprehension.

TABLE OF CONTENTS

CHAPTER 1

SNAP AND CRUNCH

A snapping turtle rests at the bottom of a murky lake. It waits for fish in the dark water. It holds its mouth open and wiggles its red tongue.

Some snapping turtles have red tongues that look like worms. The turtles use them to trick fish.

Soon, a small fish swims by. The snapping turtle holds still. It keeps its mouth open. The fish gets closer and closer.

Snapping turtles often hide near the bottom of muddy lakes and rivers.

FAST FACT

Some snapping turtles hide under mud or plants.

Snapping turtles can swim faster than they can walk.

Snap! The turtle's powerful jaws clamp shut. It eats the fish. Then it swims to the surface. It rests in the sun.

BITING POWER

Snapping turtles have strong bites. Their mouths do not have teeth. Instead, their jaws are shaped like pointy beaks. These sharp beaks can break through bones.

CHAPTER 2

LiFE iN THE WATER

Snapping turtles are **reptiles**. There are two main kinds. Common snapping turtles have smooth shells. Alligator snapping turtles have spikes.

Alligator snapping turtles are very large. Some can weigh up to 200 pounds (91 kg).

Snapping turtles live in North and South America. They can be found in ponds, lakes, rivers, and marshes.

Common snapping turtles usually weigh between 10 and 35 pounds (4.5 and 16 kg).

Snapping turtles spend most of their time underwater. Some can swim underwater for up to 50 minutes at a time. Body parts near their mouths and rear ends help them get **oxygen** from the water.

Snapping turtles can get oxygen underwater with their mouths. But their rear ends can also help.

HIDE AND SEEK

Snapping turtles usually live in areas with lots of mud and plants. Their shells are often green or brown. These colors help them blend in and hide from **prey**.

CHAPTER 3

EATING TIME

Snapping turtles are **omnivores**. They eat water plants and **algae**. They also hunt fish, frogs, and other small animals.

Snapping turtles find most of their prey underwater.

The hooked shape of a snapping turtle's jaws helps it kill prey.

Snapping turtles usually hunt at night. They hide and wait underwater. When prey gets close, they surprise it and bite. Their strong jaws snap down.

Snapping turtles have sharp claws. They use their claws to dig and rip food.

Animals like snakes and foxes eat young snapping turtles. But adult snapping turtles don't have many **predators**. They have strong shells. And they can bite or claw.

FACING DANGER

The main threats to adult snapping turtles come from humans. Some people hunt the turtles. Others damage their **habitats**. Turtles may lose the places they live or the foods they eat.

◀ A snapping turtle's strong shell protects it from danger.

CHAPTER 4

LIFE CYCLE

Snapping turtles spend most of their time alone. When it is time to **mate**, they look for partners. They might have to travel far.

Snapping turtles usually come together to mate in the spring.

Female snapping turtles use their back legs to dig nests for their eggs.

After mating, female snapping turtles make nests. Each female usually lays between 20 and 45 eggs. Then she goes back to the water.

ROUGH LIFE

Few snapping turtles become adults. Many snapping turtle eggs get eaten by predators. Baby turtles also face danger. When they hatch, their shells are soft. The shells harden as they grow.

Common snapping turtle eggs are about the size of ping-pong balls.

Newly hatched snapping turtles are just 1 inch (2.5 cm) long.

The eggs hatch a few months later. The baby turtles are on their own. They move toward the water. There, they will eat and grow.

FAST FACT

Snapping turtles can live up to 45 years in the wild.

COMPREHENSION
QUESTIONS

Write your answers on a separate piece of paper.

1. Write a few sentences describing how snapping turtles hunt for food.

2. Would you be scared if you met a snapping turtle in the wild? Why or why not?

3. Which type of snapping turtle has spikes on its shell?

    A. alligator snapping turtle

    B. baby snapping turtle

    C. common snapping turtle

4. Why are baby snapping turtles more likely to be eaten by predators?

    A. Their soft shells are easier to bite through.

    B. Their dark colors are easier to see.

    C. Their small legs can move faster.

5. What does **murky** mean in this book?

*A snapping turtle rests at the bottom of a **murky** lake. It waits for fish in the dark water.*

    A. dark and dirty
    B. clear and bright
    C. hot and dry

6. What does **threats** mean in this book?

*The main **threats** to adult snapping turtles come from humans. Some people hunt the turtles.*

    A. food
    B. dangers
    C. help

Answer key on page 32.

GLOSSARY

algae
Tiny plant-like living things that are found in the water.

habitats
The places where animals normally live.

mate
To form a pair and come together to have babies.

omnivores
Animals that eat both plants and animals.

oxygen
A type of gas that animals need to breathe to survive.

predators
Animals that hunt and eat other animals.

prey
Animals that are hunted and eaten by other animals.

reptiles
Cold-blooded animals that have scales.

TO LEARN MORE

BOOKS

Amin, Anita Nahta. *Is It a Turtle or a Tortoise?* North
    Mankato, MN: Capstone Press, 2022.
Murray, Julie. *Turtles*. Minneapolis: Abdo Publishing, 2020.
Tobler, Elise. *Snapping Turtles Eat Anything!* New York:
    Enslow Publishing, 2021.

ONLINE RESOURCES

Visit **www.apexeditions.com** to find links and resources
related to this title.

ABOUT THE AUTHOR

Shannon Jade writes both fiction and nonfiction books. She
lives in Australia alongside some of the world's greatest
landscapes and most amazing animals.

INDEX

ANSWER KEY:
1. Answers will vary; 2. Answers will vary; 3. A; 4. A; 5. A; 6. B